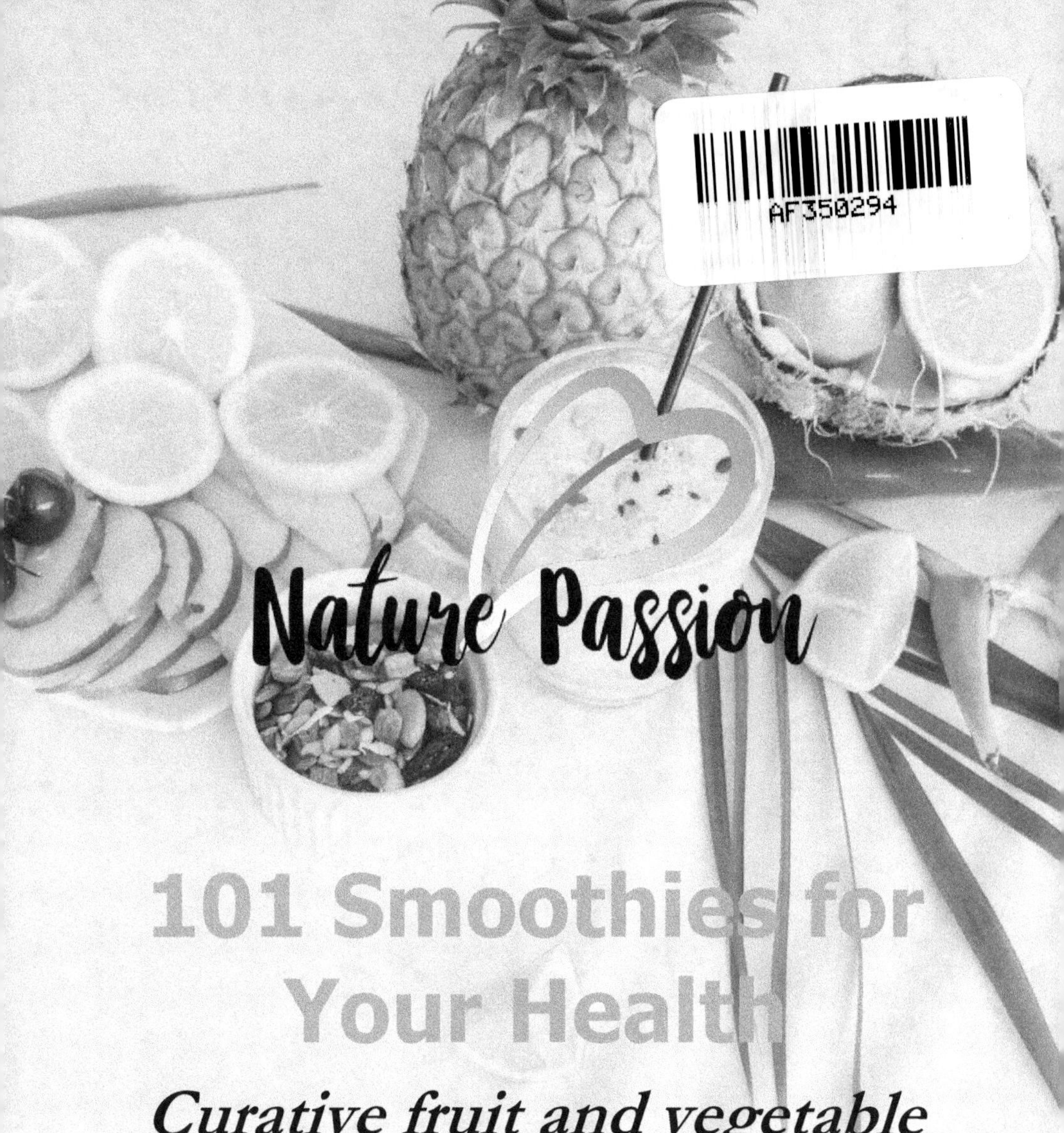

Nature Passion

101 Smoothies for Your Health

Curative fruit and vegetable smoothies recipes

Cristina & Olivier Rebiere

Table of Contents

Welcome

We welcome you in your new *Nature Passion* "**101 Smoothies for Your Health - Curative fruit and vegetable smoothies recipes**" a practical guide that we hope will help you better know the properties of fruits and vegetables. This will give you maybe the wish to start concocting curative smoothies to boost your health ;-)

I have always been fascinated by plants and their properties and often used them to treat myself, my family and even my friends.

I discovered smoothies and curative juices during our last trip to Mexico. In Mexico City, there are plenty of bars that offer this kind of juice while having their properties and virtues written on their boards.

In this guide, I will first present you the nutrients of some of the most common fruits and vegetables, and then I will propose two or three combinations that will make you feel good for each condition. I will not make an exhaustive list of conditions, but those that affect the most people.

I imagine that, like me, you do not have an infallible memory. This guide therefore allows you to remember quickly what fruits and vegetables will help you if your blood circulation problems cause you concern, if you have cholesterol problems, if you are a victim of an anemia or if you have just simply a low energy...

 **Attention**, smoothies will not heal you and certainly do not take the place of a medicine doctor's recommendations. However, fruits and vegetables are an invaluable source of vitamins, minerals and other nutrients..

Note that I do not pretend to present all the vegetables and fruits that exist because I should write a whole encyclopedia! However, I have already written another small guide in this **Nature Passion** collection: "Exotic fruits and vegetables" where I also presented the virtues of more exotic fruits. If you are interested by the subject, you can find other books here, but also on other online eBook platforms.

If natural drinks interest you, I have written other **Nature Passion** guides about herbal teas and the fresh curative juices that you can use to please you, but also to cure your little life problems. I always prefer a herbal tea, a juice or a smoothie to treat me rather than medicines and it works.

Life is full of simple pleasures that can easily turn into pure happiness ;-)...

Fruits and vegetables are very beneficial to your health, as you may already know. You eat probably already raw fruit and vegetables, in salads or in various dishes.

There are several ways to prepare juices; as " smoothie " for those who prefer the creamy drinks or as fresh juices for those who do not like the pulp of fruits and / or vegetables.

The smoothies can be made with a blender as you certainly know. You can also make milkshakes from fruits, but of course they will contain more calories than the smoothies.

Some tips for your smoothies:

- ✓ Depending on the consistency you like for your drink, add water to your smoothie if you prefer it to be more liquid.
- ✓ If you want a refreshing beverage, you can add ice cubes directly in your blender in the same time with the fruits.
- ✓ If you like sparkling drinks, then add sparkling mineral water.
- ✓ If you like iced teas, then instead of the water add cold tea and ice cubes - you'll see it's not bad at all ;-)!

 You should know that when you make a smoothie, you will put in your blender fruits and vegetables. The pulp remains in the drink, the fibers also.

The fresh juice is made using an electric fruit and vegetable juicer extractor. There are also special ones for citrus, but the one I recommend is in the photo.

It is really efficient to make fresh juice from fruits and vegetables and has the advantage that it separates the pulp from the juice as you can see, even in the picture. The juice goes in the right container and the pulp in the large black container on the left. Another advantage is that the juice is quickly absorbed by your body and consequently all its nutrients, enzymes and antioxidants.

But what is there in fruits and vegetables that can help us strengthen our health?

vitamins...

which are organic substances necessary for our body. To remind you the vitamins roles:

- ✓ **vitamin A**: stimulates growth, improves vision, helps skin hydration
- ✓ **Vitamin B complex**: comprises several vitamins that have mainly a role in the metabolism of carbohydrates, lipids and proteins, but also in the synthesis of certain hormones
- ✓ **vitamin C**: required in the synthesis of collagen and red blood cells, and stimulates the natural immune system, antioxidant and anti-scurvy
- ✓ **vitamin D**: necessary during infancy to prevent rickets, reduces the risk of osteoporosis
- ✓ **vitamin E**: is antioxidant, has a protective action on red blood cells and a beneficial effect on cholesterol
- ✓ **vitamin K**: helps the binding of calcium by the bones and has an anti-hemorrhagic effect

enzymes ...

which are complex substances that help our bodies to digest and absorb food

that protect organic molecules, for example fats or DNA from oxidation and seem to play a protective role against carcinogenesis.

 The **benefits of vegetables** are undeniable, but not always known. You already know that they are excellent sources of vitamins, which are essential for the smooth running of biochemical reactions that take place in our body.

The benefits of vegetables don't just stop at their nutritional value, but have many other benefits. Here are some of them:

- ✓ **reduced risk of diabetes**, especially type 2 diabetes, and obesity, as proven by several studies such as this one, which shows that these risks are reduced for people with a vegetarian diet.
- ✓ **excellent source of fibre** that facilitates intestinal transit, preventing constipation and reducing the risk of intestinal diseases or colon cancer. Their consumption reduces the risk of cardiovascular diseases, which are the leading cause of death worldwide. These benefits of vegetables but also of fruits have been the subject of many studies that have highlighted the virtues of vegetables.
- ✓ **reduction of bad cholesterol levels** thanks to the fibers they contain, such as pectins and certain hemicelluloses, which limit the assimilation of cholesterol. Thus, the richest in fiber are leeks, peas, celery, cabbage, corn, carrots, fennel, etc. The effect of this decrease is also due to their richness in antioxidants that would prevent the oxidation of cholesterol which is no longer deposited in the arteries, thus limiting the risk of developing cardiovascular disease.
- ✓ this has a **good effect on bones** because they are a significant source of calcium, such as broccoli, which is very rich in it, but also cabbage, endives, white beans, etc. They also contain potassium which regulates calcium

losses from the body, fighting bone demineralization and helping to prevent osteoporosis.
- ✓ this has a **beneficial effect on the skin** and its anti-aging effect, thanks in particular to carotenoids, such as beta-carotene, known for its antioxidant properties that help neutralize free radicals. Vegetables rich in beta-carotene are primarily carrots (especially raw), but also cooked sweet potato, fresh parsley, tomatoes and dandelion.
- ✓ a **favourable effect on anaemia** such as eggplants, beets.

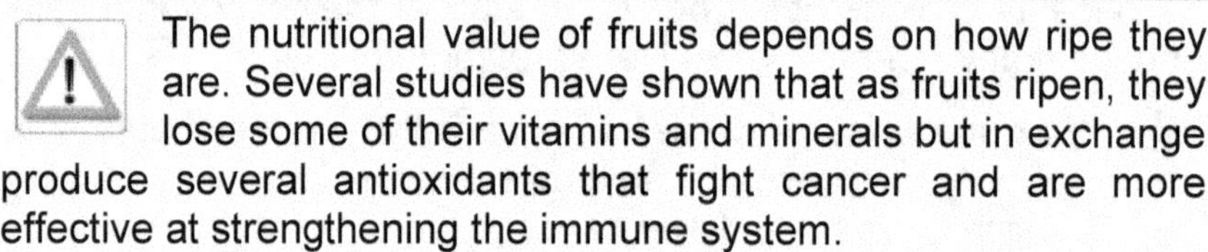

The nutritional value of fruits depends on how ripe they are. Several studies have shown that as fruits ripen, they lose some of their vitamins and minerals but in exchange produce several antioxidants that fight cancer and are more effective at strengthening the immune system.

Over the past thirty years, more than 200 studies have analyzed the relationship between fruit and vegetable consumption and cancer. The majority concludes that they have a protective effect against cancers, including those of the upper aerodigestive tract, stomach, lung and colon-rectum. This beneficial effect can be explained by the components found in fruits and vegetables: vitamins, fibre, minerals and other trace elements that act synergistically.

According to some studies, the consumption of vegetables and fruits also has a protective effect against cognitive and mental disorders and even Alzheimer's disease, as shown by this study.

Some, such as peppers, corn or spinach, contain lutein, a carotenoid that has a beneficial effect for eye disorders and the preservation of crystallized intelligence, which is the ability to use skills and knowledge acquired over the course of life.

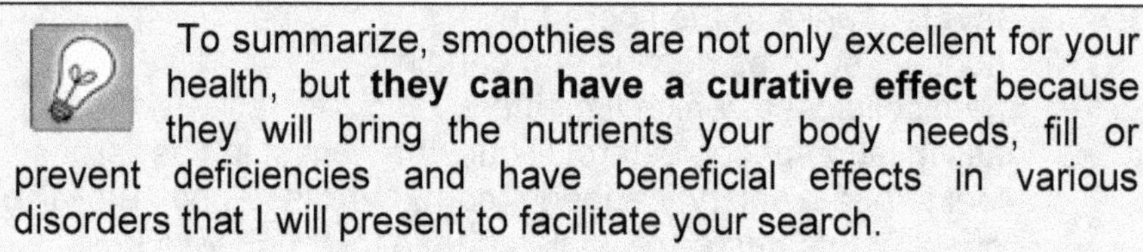

To summarize, smoothies are not only excellent for your health, but **they can have a curative effect** because they will bring the nutrients your body needs, fill or prevent deficiencies and have beneficial effects in various disorders that I will present to facilitate your search.

I will start first by introducing nutrients and medicinal properties of some fruits and vegetables in the following chapter.

Apple

Nutritional elements: The apple is rich in vitamin C (especially in its skin), but also contains vitamin A, B, K and E. It has a lot of potassium, but also iron, magnesium, calcium, phosphorus, sodium, copper and zinc.

Medicinal virtues: The apple is a diuretic, laxative and acts as an intestinal antiseptic. It is beneficial against rheumatism, anemia, gout, obesity, insomnia.

Apricot

Nutritional elements: The apricot contains vitamin A, B, C and E. It is rich in potassium, calcium and phosphorus. It also contains iron, magnesium, iodine.

It contains flavonoids that are anti-inflammatory and antioxidants.

Medicinal virtues: The apricot has beneficial effects on vision and is a rich source of antioxidants that help to remove toxins from the body and also have a good effect on the skin. The large amount of fiber is beneficial for the heart, reducing bad cholesterol. Apricots are fruits that help when you want to diet because they have few calories.

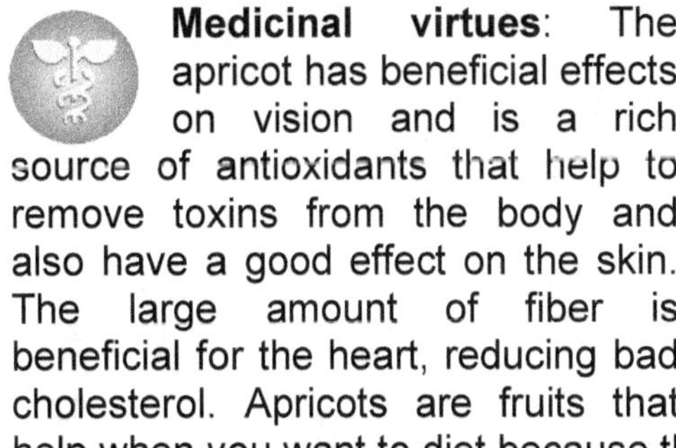

Avocado

Nutritional elements: The avocado contains vitamin A, B, C, K and E. It is rich in copper, potassium, iron, phosphorus and magnesium. It contains antioxidants and is very high in fiber.

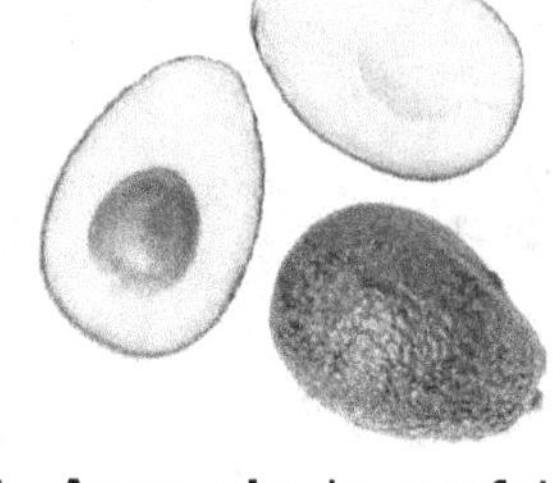

Medicinal virtues: Avocado has beneficial effects on vision and on the liver. The large amount of fiber is beneficial to the heart, reducing bad cholesterol. It ensures good intestinal transit. **Avocado** is useful during cures to stabilize weights because it ensures a quick feeling of satiety.

Banana

Nutritional elements: Banana contains vitamin B and C. It is rich in potassium, manganese, copper and magnesium. Bananas contain antioxidants.

Medicinal virtues: You may already know the bananas' properties or at least some of them. It is the only fruit I know that can be used both to facilitate intestinal transit (ripe fruit) and to treat diarrhea (not too ripe fruit). Banana also relieves intestinal burns. It is also a good antidepressant and helps to regulate stress. Banana is rich in potassium, vitamins (especially B) and iron (very useful for treating anemia).

Beetroot

Nutritional elements: Beetroot contains vitamin B9 and C and leaves have vitamin A. The beetroot is rich in potassium, manganese, iodine and phosphorus.

Beetroots are also sources of fiber, folate and antioxidants.

Medicinal virtues: Beetroot has beneficial effects for diseases related to digestion and blood. It controls the tension, detoxifies the liver, stimulates the immune system and red blood cell production.

Bell Pepper

Nutritional elements: The bell pepper is rich in vitamin A, B, C and K. It contains a lot of fibers and few calories.

It contains luteolin that activates neural circuits involved in learning.

Medicinal virtues: Pepper prevents the development of cancer and is excellent for the memory. It is also beneficial in digestive disorders, especially for cramps and colic.

Blueberries

Nutritional elements: Blueberries are rich in vitamin A, B and C. They contain magnesium, copper, chromium and zinc.

Blueberries are among the fruits with very good antioxidant properties.

Medicinal virtues: Fresh blueberries have laxative properties. They calm colitis and are beneficial in infectious diarrhea and gastroenteric disorders. They also reduce the risk of cardiovascular diseases and cancer. Blueberries strengthen the immune system. Infusion of blueberry leaves is beneficial for diabetes.

Carrot

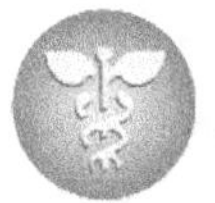

Nutritional elements: Carrots contain vitamin A, B, C, D, E and K. They are rich in calcium, potassium, magnesium, iron and phosphorus.

Carrots are also sources of antioxidants.

 **Medicinal virtues**: Carrot purifies the blood, improves vision, disinfects the intestines, combat obesity, depression, skin problems and intestinal worms.

Celery

 **Nutritional elements**: Celery contains vitamin A, B and C. Celery is low in calories.

Medicinal virtues: Celery cleanses the blood, helps increasing the red blood cells. It is useful to combat constipation, migraines, and rheumatism. Celery has diuretic and tonic properties. It is also beneficial in cases of hypertension, in bronchial ailments and fights stress with a relaxing effect on the nervous system.

Cucumber

Nutritional elements: Cucumber contains vitamin A, B, C and E. It is a source of calcium, phosphorus, magnesium and potassium. Cucumbers are also sources of folic acid.

Medicinal virtues: Cucumbers help the functioning of kidneys, have a beneficial effect on the skin, rheumatism and gout. This is an excellent detoxifier and is used in weight-loss program. It is also beneficial in cases of hypertension, in muscle diseases.

Grapes

Nutritional elements: Grapes are rich in vitamin A, B and C, but also contains vitamin B, K and E. It contains a lot of potassium, but also calcium, phosphorus, magnesium, iron and copper.

Grapes are very low in saturated fat, cholesterol and sodium. It has a high sugar content and contains polyphenols which are antioxidants.

Medicinal virtues: In the skin of red grapes there is resveratrol, an antioxidant that has anti-inflammatory properties that can reduce allergic symptoms. Grapes are rich in fiber and minerals that have laxative properties, diuretic and detoxifying. They are excellent for detoxification cures and have a beneficial effect for allergies. They also stimulate the liver.

Kiwi

Nutritional elements: The kiwi is very rich in vitamin C and also contains vitamin A, B, E and K. It is rich in potassium, phosphorus and magnesium, but contains also copper, calcium, iron and zinc.

Kiwi is one of fruits having the highest antioxidant properties.

Medicinal virtues: Kiwi reduces cardiovascular risks. It is beneficial in the treatments of weight loss because it has few calories and is high in fiber.

Lemon

Nutritional elements: Lemon contains a lot of vitamin C, but also vitamins A, B and E. It is rich in calcium, potassium, magnesium, iron and zinc. Lemons are also sources of antioxidants

Medicinal virtues: Lemon is antiviral, antibacterial, recommended in heart and liver diseases, combat obesity and hair loss. It is also diuretic.

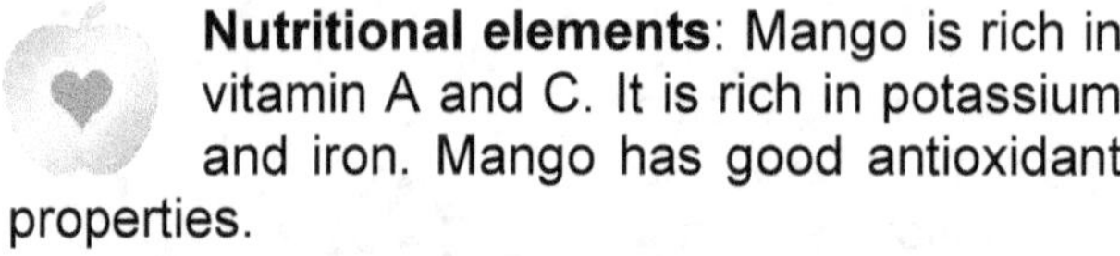

Mango

Nutritional elements: Mango is rich in vitamin A and C. It is rich in potassium and iron. Mango has good antioxidant properties.

Medicinal virtues: Mango juice is recommended as a fortifier. The majority of mangoes contain cellulosic fibers that regulate intestinal transit.

Melon

Nutritional elements: The melon is rich in vitamin A, and also contains vitamin B and C. It is rich in calcium and potassium, but has also phosphorus, iron and magnesium.

The melon is one of fruits with very good antioxidant properties. It contains adenosine which prevents the formation of blood clots.

Medicinal virtues: Melon helps eliminating intestinal parasites. It is diuretic and beneficial for rheumatism and gout.

Orange

Nutritional elements: Orange is rich in vitamin C but also contains vitamin A, B, K and E. It has a lot of potassium, but also contains calcium, phosphorus iron, copper and zinc.

The orange contains antioxidants.

Medicinal virtues: The orange is beneficial for nausea, rheumatism, respiratory diseases and skin, anemia, insomnia and asthma.

Peach

Nutritional elements: Peach is rich in vitamin A, B, C and E. It also contains iron, magnesium, phosphorus, iodine, potassium, selenium and zinc. Peach contains antioxidants.

Medicinal virtues: Peach has a good energizing effect, stimulates appetite, facilitates intestinal transit and helps to balance the nervous system. It is diuretic, laxative and strengthens the immune system of the organism.

Parsley

Nutritional elements: Parsley leaves are rich in vitamin A and C. Parsley contains calcium, iron, magnesium, phosphorus, sodium, potassium.

Medicinal virtues: The parsley root is diuretic, anthelmintic. Its action is good for asthenia, anorexia, hypertension, arthritis and rheumatism.

Pear

Nutritional elements: Pears are rich in vitamin A, B, C, K and E. They contain a lot of potassium, but also have iron, phosphorus, calcium, copper and zinc. The pear contains antioxidants.

Medicinal virtues: The pear has few calories and is good in weight loss cures, facilitates intestinal transit and is beneficial for the eyes. It is diuretic, anti-inflammatory and laxative. It helps to balance the nervous system, has calming and sedative effects.

Pineapple

Nutritional elements: Pineapple contains vitamin A, B, C and K. It is rich in calcium and magnesium. It also contains potassium, phosphorus, sodium and iron. It contains also bromelain which has cicatrizing and anti-inflammatory effect.

Medicinal virtues: Pineapple is diuretic, laxative and anti-inflammatory. It is recommended for gout and rheumatism.

Pitaya, the dragon fruit

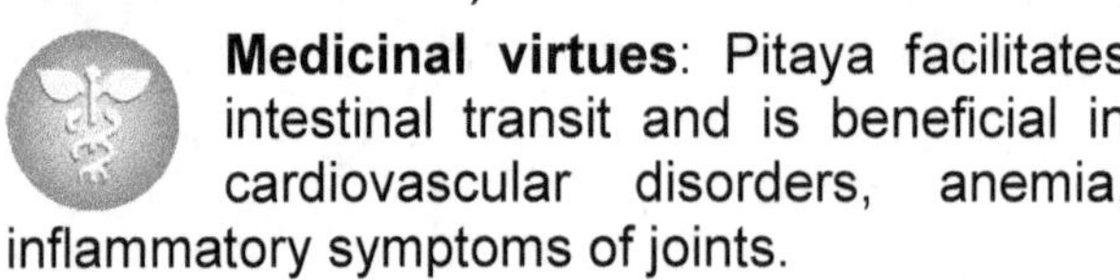

Nutritional elements: Dragon fruit is rich in vitamins, minerals, fibers, antioxidants and betacyanine (especially the red-fleshed variety, which is less rich in vitamins).

Medicinal virtues: Pitaya facilitates intestinal transit and is beneficial in cardiovascular disorders, anemia, inflammatory symptoms of joints.

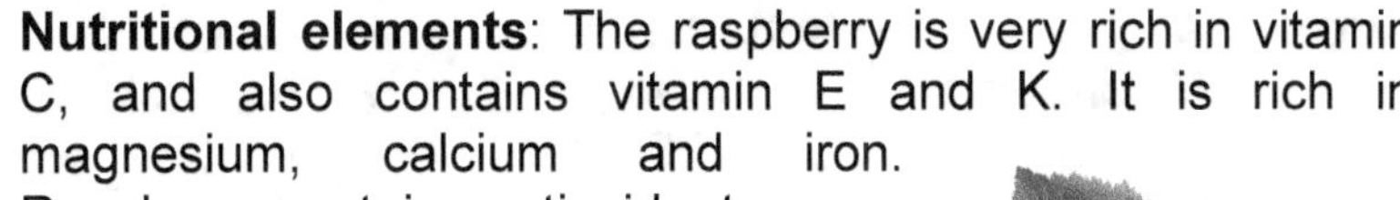

Raspberry

Nutritional elements: The raspberry is very rich in vitamin C, and also contains vitamin E and K. It is rich in magnesium, calcium and iron. Raspberry contains antioxidants.

Medicinal virtues: Raspberries facilitate intestinal transit, reduce cardiovascular and cancer risks. They are beneficial in slimming cures.

Strawberry

Nutritional elements: The The strawberry is very rich in vitamin C, and also contains vitamin E and K. It is rich in potassium, calcium, manganese and magnesium.

Medicinal virtues: Strawberries reduce cardiovascular and cancer risks. They are beneficial in slimming cures because they have few calories and lots of water.

Tomato

Nutritional elements: Tomatoes are rich in vitamins A, B, D, E and K. It contains a lot of potassium, but also has iron, calcium, phosphorus, sodium and iodine. The tomato contains lycopene which has an antioxidant effect.

Medicinal virtues: Tomato is good for rheumatism, indigestion. It prevents cardiovascular disease. The tomato has diuretic and detoxifying properties.

Watermelon

Nutritional elements: Watermelon is rich in vitamin A, B, C, D and E. It is rich in calcium and magnesium, but also contains phosphorus, iron and zinc.

Watermelon contains lycopene which has an antioxidant effect. It has few calories.

Medicinal virtues: Watermelon is an excellent detoxifier and is used in weight-loss program. It prevents heart, respiratory and degenerative problems. It is diuretic and beneficial for diseases of the kidneys.

Zucchini

Nutritional elements: Zucchini is very rich in vitamin A, but also contains vitamin C, B1 and B6, E and K. It is rich in phosphorus, magnesium, copper, calcium and zinc.

Zucchinis are also sources of antioxidants and folic acid.

Medicinal virtues: The zucchini stimulates digestion because it is rich in fiber, reduces heart risks and stroke. It is beneficial for lowering blood pressure. It is also a gastric dressing useful in gastric disorders and ulcers. It has an anti-inflammatory role for rheumatism and arthritis.

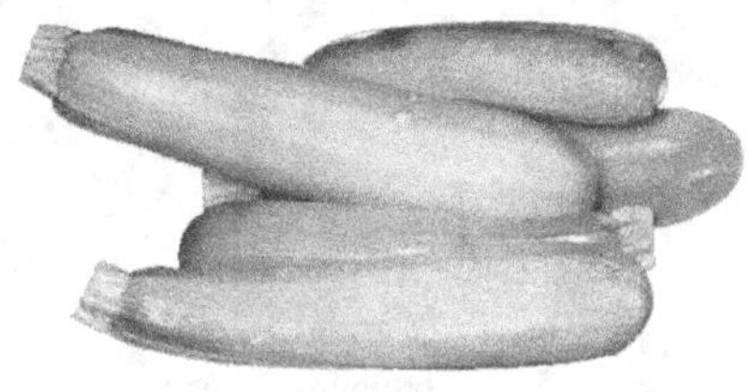

 Acne is a skin condition that occurs in adolescence and is linked to the hypersecretion of sebum. We've all experienced the embarrassment and also the embarrassment caused by the pimples that "bloom" on our face as teenagers.

Well, this problem may continue to appear even later. So, if you want to prevent or minimize the effects of acne, here are some smoothies that will do you or your teens good.

Recipe 1 – Tomato, Apple & Cucumber Smoothie

- 2 ripe tomatoes
- 1 apple and 1 cucumber

 Wash the tomatoes, apple and cucumber thoroughly. Peel them, including the tomatoes, and remove the core from the apple. Blend everything in a blender.

Recipe 2 – Banana, Cucumber & Raspberry Smoothie

- 1 banana, 10 raspberries
- 1 cucumber

 Wash the raspberries, banana and cucumber thoroughly. Peel the banana and cucumber. Blend everything in a blender.

Recipe 3 – Apple Pineapple Smoothie

- 2 apples
- and a few slices of fresh pineapple

 Wash the apples thoroughly. Peel the pineapple and add as many slices as you'd like. Peel the apples and remove their cores. Blend everything in a blender.

Recipe 4 – Avocado and Pineapple Smoothie

- 1 avocado
- And a few slices of fresh pineapple

Wash the avocado well and remove the pit. Peel the pineapple and add as many slices as you'd like. Blend everything in a blender.

 Allergy is a phenomenon of pathological exaggeration of the immune response, especially the inflammatory response.

It's an increasingly prevalent condition, so boost your immune system with smoothies.

Recipe 5 – Carrot, Cucumber & Apple Smoothie

- 1 carrot
- 1 cucumber
- 1 apple

 Wash the carrot, apple and cucumber thoroughly. Peel them and remove the core from the apple. Blend everything in a blender.

Recipe 6 – Pear and Raisin Smoothie

- 2 pears
- and a bunch of black grapes

 Wash the pears and grapes thoroughly. Peel the pears and remove the cores. Blend everything in a blender.

> Anemia is an abnormality of the blood count characterized by a decrease in hemoglobin levels. Here are some smoothies that may be beneficial if you suffer from anemia.

Recipe 7 – Carrot Pitaya & Orange Smoothie

- 2 carrots
- 1 pitaya
- 1 orange

Wash the fruit thoroughly. Peel the fruit and cut off the ends of the carrots. Blend everything in a blender.

Recipe 8 – Apple, Lemon & Orange Smoothie

- 2 apples
- 1 lemon
- 2 oranges

Wash the fruit thoroughly. Peel them and remove the cores from the apples. Blend everything in a blender.

Recipe 9 – Banana & Orange Smoothie

- 1 banana
- 2 oranges

Wash the oranges and banana thoroughly. Peel them. Blend everything in a blender.

Smoothies for cellulite

Cellulite is the result of the distribution of adipose tissue, increased in the skin of certain regions characteristic of women. This increase is especially noticeable in the thighs, buttocks and hips and in the appearance of orange peel skin.

Here are some smoothies that may be beneficial in reducing cellulite.

Recipe 10 – Pineapple, Celery & Carrot Smoothie

- a few pieces of pineapple
- 1 carrot
- 1 celery stalk

Wash the celery and carrot thoroughly. Peel the pineapple and carrot. Blend everything in a blender.

Recipe 11 – Apple & Carrot Smoothie

- 2 carrots
- 2 apples

Wash the apples and carrots thoroughly. Peel them and remove the cores from the apples. Blend everything in a blender.

Recipe 12 – Beetroot & Orange Smoothie

- 1 beetroot
- 2 oranges

Wash the beetroot and oranges thoroughly. Peel them. Blend everything in a blender. Be careful because beetroot stains!!

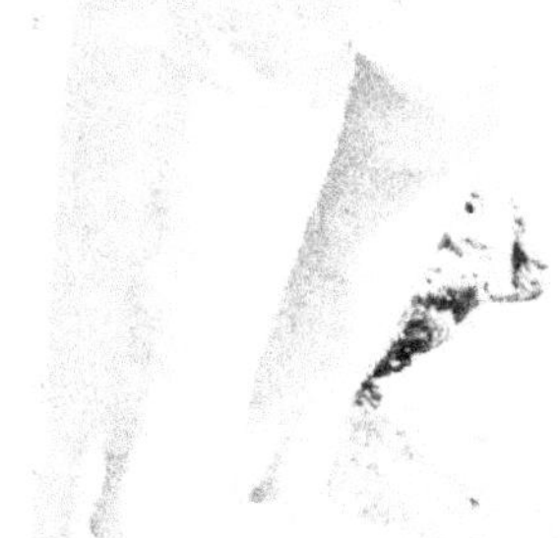

Here are some recipes to tone your hair and scalp!

Recipe 13 – Kiwi, Orange & Lemon Smoothie

- 2 kiwis
- 1 orange
- 1 lemon

Wash the fruit thoroughly. Peel them.

Blend everything in a blender.

Recipe 14 – Apple, Pepper & Orange Smoothie

- 2 apples
- 1 red bell pepper
- 1 orange

Wash the apples, pepper and orange thoroughly. Peel the orange and apples. Remove the core from the apples and pepper. Blend everything in a blender.

Recipe 15 – Kiwi, Parsley & Orange Smoothie

- 1 kiwi
- 1 parsley
- 2 oranges

Wash the kiwi, oranges and parsley (root and a few leaves) thoroughly. Peel the oranges, kiwi and parsley. Blend everything in a blender.

 Many of us have problems with blood circulation. The heat is an aggravating factor and our legs suffer during the summer... Because of the stagnation of blood in the lower part of the body, the heat causes the veins to dilate, which can weaken the lining of the veins, compromising their elasticity in the long run.

Here are some smoothies that can be beneficial by thinning the blood and strengthening the veins.

Recipe 16 – Beetroot, Kiwi & Orange Smoothie

- 1 beetroot
- 2 kiwis
- 1 orange

 Wash the beetroot, kiwis and orange thoroughly. Peel them. Blend everything in a blender.

Recipe 17 – Melon, Grape & Celery Smoothie

- 1/2 melon
- 1 bunch of grapes
- 1 celery

 Wash the melon, grapes and celery thoroughly. Peel the celery and melon. Blend everything in a blender.

Recipe 18 – Melon & Orange Smoothie

- 1 small melon
- 1 orange

 Wash the melon and orange thoroughly. Peel them and cut the melon into large cubes. Blend everything in a blender.

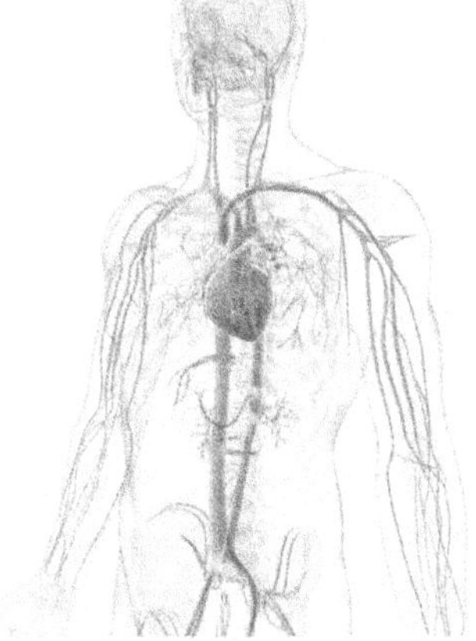

Recipe 19 – Strawberry, Mango & Orange Smoothie

- 1 mango
- 1 orange
- 6 strawberries

Wash the mango, strawberries and orange thoroughly. Peel the mango and remove the pit. Peel the orange. Blend everything in a blender.

Recipe 20 – Pear, Apricot & Orange Smoothie

- 2 pears
- 2 apricots
- 6 strawberries

Wash the pears, apricots and orange thoroughly. Peel the pears and remove the core and pit from the apricots. Peel the orange. Blend everything in a blender.

Here are some smoothies that may be beneficial for fighting bad cholesterol.

Recipe 21 – Peach, Apricot & Orange Smoothie

- 2 peaches, 4 apricots

- 1 orange

Wash the peaches, apricots and orange thoroughly. Peel the orange and remove the pits from the peaches and apricots. Blend everything in a blender.

Recipe 22 – Avocado, Apple & Raspberry Smoothie

- 1 avocado, 1 apple

- 10 raspberries

Wash the apple, raspberries and avocado thoroughly. Peel the avocado and remove the pit. Peel the apple and remove the core. Blend everything in a blender.

Recipe 23 – Kiwi & Lemon Smoothie

- 3 kiwis

- 1 lemon

Wash the kiwis and lemon thoroughly. Peel them.

Blend everything in a blender.

Recipe 24 – Orange & Strawberry Smoothie

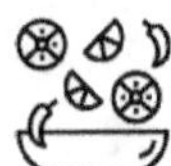

- 2 oranges
- 6 strawberries

Wash the strawberries and oranges thoroughly. Peel the oranges.

Blend everything in a blender.

Recipe 25 – Pineapple, Carrot & Walnut Smoothie

- a few slices of pineapple

- 1 carrot, 1 or 2 walnuts

Wash the carrot thoroughly. Peel it. Peel the pineapple and cut a few slices into cubes. Add the nuts. Blend everything in a blender.

Colitis is an inflammation of the colon. Here are some smoothies that may be beneficial in treating colitis.

>  **Be careful**, however, not to overdo it, as consuming too many smoothies could have the opposite effect!

Recipe 26 – Zucchini Apple Smoothie

- 2 zucchini
- 2 apples

Wash the zucchini and apples thoroughly. Peel them and remove the ends of the zucchini and the cores of the apples. Blend everything in a blender.

Recipe 27 – Carrot, Apple & Blueberry Smoothie

- 2 carrots
- 2 apples
- 100 g blueberries

Wash the carrots, blueberries and apples thoroughly. Peel the carrots and apples and remove the tips of the carrots and the cores from the apples. Blend everything in a blender.

Conjunctivitis is an inflammation of the mucous membranes around the eyelids, usually benign. It is important to see a doctor, who will prescribe antibiotic eye drops if you have a bacterial infection.

Here are some smoothies that can benefit your eyes!

Recipe 28 – Carrot, Apricot & Tomato Smoothie

- 2 carrots
- 4 apricots
- 2 tomatoes

Wash the carrots, apricots and tomatoes thoroughly. Remove the pits from the apricots. Peel the carrots and tomatoes. Blend everything in a blender.

Recipe 29 – Zucchini, Avocado & Pear Smoothie

- 1 zucchini
- 1 pear, 1 avocado

Wash the zucchini, pear and avocado thoroughly. Peel the zucchini, avocado and pear. Remove the pit from the avocado, the core from the pear and the ends from the zucchini. Blend everything in a blender.

Recipe 30 – Blueberry, Carrot & Pear Smoothie

- 100 g blueberries
- 1 pear, 1 carrot

Wash the carrot, pear and blueberries thoroughly. Peel the carrot and pear. Remove the core from the pear and the ends from the carrot. Blend everything in a blender.

Smoothies to Prevent Diabetes

Diabetes refers to a syndrome characterized by an increase in urine production, necessarily accompanied by excessive thirst. Diabetes mellitus is the most common and is related to an abnormality in insulin synthesis.

Here are a few smoothies that can prevent it from occurring:

Recipe 31 – Apple Blueberry Smoothie

- 2 apples
- 200 g blueberries

Wash the zucchini and apples thoroughly. Peel them and remove the ends of the zucchini and the cores of the apples. Blend everything in a blender.

Recipe 32 – Apple & Grape Smoothie

- 2 apples
- 1 bunch of grapes

Wash the apples and grapes thoroughly. Peel the apples and remove the core. Blend in a blender.

Recipe 33 – Pear, Carrot & Lemon Smoothie

- 3 pears, 1 carrot, 1 lemon

Wash the pears, carrot and lemon thoroughly. Peel them and remove the core from the pears and the ends from the carrot. Blend everything in a blender.

The liver has a very important role in our body. Here are some smoothies that can be beneficial for the liver.

Recipe 34 – Carrot & Grapefruit Smoothie

- 2 carrots
- 1 grapefruit

Wash the carrots and grapefruit thoroughly. Remove the ends of the carrots.

Blend everything in a blender.

Recipe 35 – Beetroot & Lemon Smoothie

- 3 beets

- 1 lemon

Wash the beets and lemon thoroughly.

Peel them. Blend everything in a blender.

Recipe 36 – Celery & Orange Smoothie

- 1 celery
- 2 oranges

Wash the celery and oranges thoroughly. Peel them.

Blend everything in a blender. Add a spoonful of olive oil to protect against oxidative damage to liver tissue.

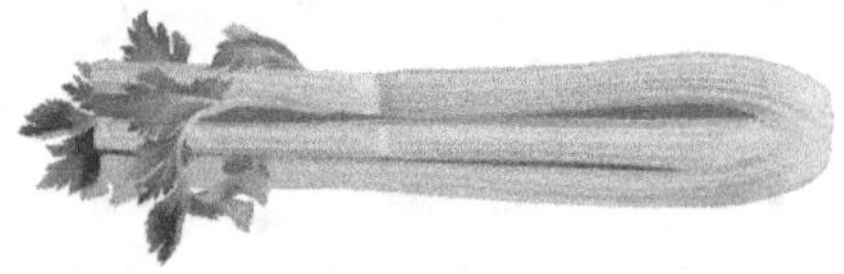

Recipe 37 – Grape, Avocado & Lemon Smoothie

- 1 bunch of grapes
- 1 avocado, 1 lemon

Wash the grapes, avocado and lemon thoroughly. Peel the avocado and lemon. Remove the pit from the avocado. Blend everything in a blender. Add a spoonful of olive oil to protect against oxidative damage to liver tissue.

Smoothies for High Blood Pressure

High blood pressure is a cardiovascular disease characterized by high blood pressure.

Here are some smoothies that can be beneficial for high blood pressure, by lowering it naturally or by preventing it:

Recipe 38 – Pear, Zucchini and Orange Smoothie

- 1 pear
- 1 zucchini
- 1 orange

Wash the pear, zucchini and orange thoroughly. Peel them and remove the core from the pear and the ends of the zucchini. Blend everything in a blender.

Recipe 39 – Banana, Parsley & Cucumber Smoothie

- 1 banana
- 1 parsley root
- 1 cucumber

Wash the banana, cucumber and parsley thoroughly.

Peel them and cut off the ends of the parsley and cucumber. Blend everything in a blender.

Recipe 40 – Celery, Grape & Beetroot Smoothie

- 1 beetroot
- 1 celery
- 1 bunch of grapes

Wash the beetroot, grapes and celery thoroughly. Peel the beetroot and celery. Blend everything in a blender.

Smoothies for Insomnia

Insomnia is represented by sleep disorders.

Here are some smoothies that can be beneficial for reducing insomnia.

Recipe 41 – Apple, Bell Pepper & Orange Smoothie

- 2 apples
- 1 bell pepper
- 1 orange

Wash the apples, pepper and orange thoroughly. Peel the orange and apples. Remove the core from the pepper and apples. Blend everything in a blender.

Recipe 42 – Banana, Orange & Strawberry Smoothie

- 1 banana
- 1 orange
- 4 strawberries

Wash the banana, orange and strawberries thoroughly. Peel the banana and orange. Blend everything in a blender.

Recipe 43 – Celery & Orange Smoothie

- 3 oranges
- 1 celery

Wash the oranges and celery thoroughly. Peel them.

Blend everything in a blender.

>  Immunity is the state of equilibrium that is characterized by adequate biological defenses to fight infection, disease, or any other biological invasion undesirable to the body.

Here are some smoothies that may be beneficial for boosting immunity.

Recipe 44 – Watermelon & Blueberry Smoothie

- 3 slices of watermelon
- 100 g blueberries

Wash the watermelon and blueberries thoroughly. Remove the skin from the watermelon.

Blend everything in a blender.

Recipe 45 – Orange Apple Smoothie

- 1 orange
- 2 apples

Wash the orange and apples thoroughly. Peel them and remove the cores from the apples.

Blend everything in a blender.

Recipe 46 – Beetroot & Peach Smoothie

- 1 beetroot
- 3 peaches

Wash the beetroot and peaches thoroughly. Peel the beetroot and remove the pit from the peaches.

Blend everything in a blender.

Recipe 47 – Apple Lemon Smoothie

- 3 apples
- 1 lemon

Wash the apples and lemon thoroughly. Peel them and remove the cores from the apples.

Blend everything in a blender.

Recipe 48 – Carrot, Orange & Celery Smoothie

- 2 carrots
- 1 orange
- 1 celery

Wash the carrots, celery and orange thoroughly. Peel them and remove the ends of the carrots. Blend everything in a blender.

Recipe 49 – Mango Orange Smoothie

- 1 mango
- 1 orange

Wash the mango and orange thoroughly. Peel them and remove the pit from the mango.

Blend everything in a blender.

Recipe 50 – Blueberry, Apple & Orange Smoothie

- 100 g blueberries
- 1 apple
- 1 orange

Wash the blueberries, apple and orange thoroughly. Peel the apple and orange and remove the core from the apple.

Blend everything in a blender, adding more water until you get the desired consistency.

Fatigue is a fairly common ailment in today's society. It can be physiological or psychological, but it diminishes us just as much... So, here are some smoothies that can be beneficial to fight fatigue and that will give you back your energy.

Recipe 51 – Melon & Apple Smoothie

- 1 melon
- 1 apple

Wash the melon and apple thoroughly. Peel them and cut the melon into large cubes. Remove the core from the apple. Blend everything in a blender.

Recipe 52 – Orange, Kiwi & Parsley Smoothie

- 1 orange
- 1 kiwi
- a few sprigs of parsley

Wash the orange, parsley and kiwi thoroughly. Peel them. Blend everything in a blender.

Recipe 53 – Clementine, Strawberry & Apricot Smoothie

- 1 clementine
- 3 apricots
- 6 strawberries

Wash the fruit thoroughly. Peel the clementine and remove the pit from the apricots.

Blend everything in a blender.

Migraine is a headache that can even cause nausea and can be quite debilitating.

Here are some smoothies that may be beneficial for migraine.

Recipe 54 – Celery, Cucumber & Lemon Smoothie

- 1 celery
- 1 cucumber
- 1 lemon
- 1 tablespoon honey

Wash the celery, cucumber and lemon thoroughly. Peel the celery, cucumber and lemon. Blend everything in a blender. Add the honey at the end.

Recipe 55 – Apple, Pear & Pineapple Smoothie

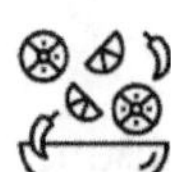

- 1 apple
- 1 pear
- 2 slices of pineapple

Wash the apple and pear thoroughly. Peel the apple and pear and remove the cores. Peel the pineapple and cut it into cubes. Blend everything in a blender.

Osteoporosis is characterized by excessive skeletal fragility, due to a decrease in bone mass. It is a condition that affects women more than men. Here are some smoothies that can benefit osteoporosis and help strengthen your bones.

Recipe 56 – Orange, Watermelon & Carrot Smoothie

- 1 orange
- 2 slices watermelon
- 1 carrot

Wash the carrot, watermelon and orange thoroughly. Peel them. Remove the ends of the carrot.

Cut the watermelon into large cubes. Blend everything in a blender.

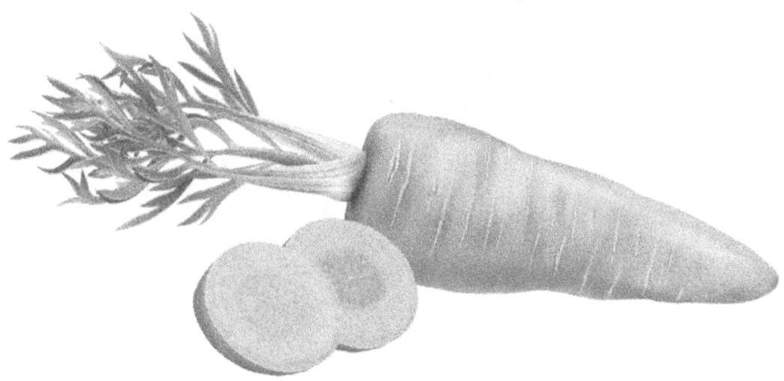

Recipe 57 – Apple, Orange & Kiwi Smoothie

- 1 apple
- 1 orange
- 1 kiwi

Wash the apple, orange and kiwi thoroughly. Peel the fruit and remove the core from the apple.

Blend everything in a blender.

Recipe 58 – Avocado, Cucumber & Orange Smoothie

- 1 avocado
- 1/2 cucumber
- 1 orange

Wash the avocado, cucumber and orange thoroughly. Peel them and remove the pit from the avocado. Blend everything in a blender. Add a spoonful of olive oil.

Recipe 59 – Banana & Tomato Smoothie

- 1 banana
- 2 tomatoes

Wash the banana and tomatoes thoroughly. Remove the tomato and banana peels. Blend everything in a blender.

Intestinal parasites are parasites that occupy the digestive tract. Here are some smoothies that may be beneficial in combating them.

Recipe 60 – Melon, Lemon & Carrot Smoothie

- 1 melon
- 1 carrot
- 1 lemon

Wash the carrot, lemon and melon thoroughly. Peel them and remove the ends of the carrot. Blend everything in a blender.

Recipe 61 – Parsley, Celery & Lime Smoothie

- 1 parsley root
- 1 celery
- 2 limes

Wash the parsley, celery and lemons thoroughly. Peel them. Blend everything in a blender. Add a little honey.

Recipe 62 – Pineapple, Celery & Orange Smoothie

- 3 pineapple slices
- 1 celery
- 1 orange

Wash the pineapple, celery and orange thoroughly. Peel them. Blend everything in a blender.

The gallbladder is an organ that sits in the abdomen against the liver. The main function of the gallbladder is to store bile for release during digestion. Several conditions can affect this organ.

Here are some smoothies that may be beneficial for gallbladder conditions.

Recipe 63 – Carrot Cucumber Smoothie

- 2 carrots
- 1 cucumber

Wash the carrots and cucumber thoroughly. Peel them off and remove the ends. Blend everything in a blender.

Recipe 64 – Grape, Carrot & Celery Smoothie

- 1 bunch of grapes
- 1 celery
- 1 carrot

Wash the grapes, carrots and celery thoroughly. Peel the celery and carrot and cut off the ends of the carrots. Blend everything in a blender.

Recipe 65 – Beetroot, Carrot & Lemon Smoothie

- 1 beetroot
- 1 carrot
- 1 lemon

Wash the beetroot, carrot and lemon thoroughly. Peel them. Blend everything in a blender.

As you know, the heart is our vital organ and therefore the one that needs to be taken care of the most.

Here are some smoothies that can be beneficial in protecting and strengthening your heart.

Recipe 66 – Melon, Lemon & Carrot Smoothie

- 2 pears,
- 1 lemon,
- 2 kiwis

Wash the carrot, lemon and melon thoroughly. Peel them and remove the ends of the carrot. Blend in a blender.

Recipe 67 – Melon & Zucchini Smoothie

- 1/2 melon
- 2 zucchini

Wash the zucchini and melon thoroughly. Peel them. Blend everything in a blender.

Recipe 68 – Watermelon & Tomato Smoothie

- 2 slices of watermelon
- 2-3 tomatoes

Wash the watermelon and tomatoes thoroughly. Peel the skin off the watermelon and cut two slices into cubes. Blend everything in a blender.

Recipe 69 – Pitaya & Kiwi Smoothie

- 1 pitaya
- 2 kiwis

Wash the fruit thoroughly. Peel them.

Blend everything in a blender.

Recipe 70 – Melon & Strawberry Smoothie

- 1 melon
- 5 strawberries

Wash the strawberries and melon thoroughly.

Peel the melon and cut it into cubes. Blend everything in a blender.

A respiratory condition affects the respiratory system or causes breathing problems.

Here are some smoothies that can be beneficial for respiratory ailments and will strengthen your lungs.

Recipe 71 – Carrot, Basil & Orange Smoothie

- 2 carrots
- 1 orange
- 4 fresh basil leaves

Wash the carrots, basil and orange thoroughly. Peel the carrots and orange and cut off the ends of the carrots.

Blend everything in a blender.

Recipe 72 – Watermelon Lemon Smoothie

- 1/2 watermelon
- 1 lemon

Wash the watermelon and lemon thoroughly. Peel them and cut the watermelon into cubes.

Blend everything in a blender.

Recipe 73 – Apple & Tomato Smoothie

- 2 apples
- 2 tomatoes

Wash the apples and tomatoes thoroughly. Remove the core from the apples.

Blend everything in a blender.

Rheumatism affects the joints and connective tissues.

Osteoarthritis is a disease that affects the joints, causing painful pain and discomfort.

Here are some smoothies that can be beneficial for rheumatism, osteoarthritis and strengthen your joints.

Recipe 74 – Parsley, Apple & Orange Smoothie

- 1 parsley
- 1 apple
- 1 orange

Wash the parsley, apple and orange thoroughly. Peel them, remove the core from the apple and cut off the ends of the parsley. Blend everything in a blender.

Recipe 75 – Tomato, Celery & Carrot Smoothie

- 3 tomatoes
- 1 celery
- 1 carrot

Wash the tomatoes, celery and carrot thoroughly. Peel the celery and carrot and cut off the ends of the carrot.

Blend everything in a blender. Add a spoonful of olive oil as it has a protective role for the joints.

Recipe 76 – Pineapple Orange Smoothie

- several slices of pineapple
- 1 orange

Wash the orange thoroughly. Peel the pineapple and orange.

Blend everything in a blender.

Recipe 77 – Melon & Cucumber Smoothie

- 1/2 melon
- 1 cucumber

Wash the cucumber and melon thoroughly.

Peel them. Blend everything in a blender.

Excess weight is one of the problems of our century. Here are some smoothies that can be fighting obesity and be beneficial in weight loss cures.

Recipe 78 – Melon, Lemon & Carrot Smoothie

- 2-3 watermelon slices,
- 1 cucumber,
- 1 carrot

Wash the watermelon, cucumber and carrot thoroughly. Peel them and cut them into pieces. Blend everything in a blender.

Recipe 79 – Avocado, Orange & Pear Smoothie

- 1 avocado,
- 1 pear
- 1 orange

Wash the avocado, pear and orange thoroughly. Peel them and remove the pit from the avocado and the core from the pear. Blend everything in a blender.

Recipe 80 – Apple, Strawberry & Kiwi Smoothie

- 1 apple,
- 5 strawberries
- 2 kiwis

Wash the strawberries, apple and kiwi thoroughly. Peel the apple and kiwis and remove the core from the apple. Blend everything in a blender.

Recipe 81 – Apple, Carrot & Orange Smoothie

- 1 apple,
- 2 carrots
- 1 orange

Wash the carrots, apple and orange thoroughly. Peel them and remove the core from the apple. Blend everything in a blender.

Recipe 82 – Raspberry, Apple & Kiwi Smoothie

- 150 g raspberries,
- 1 apple,
- 1 kiwi

Wash the raspberries, apple and kiwi thoroughly. ;P peel the apple and kiwi and remove the core from the apple. Blend everything in a blender.

You all know, of course, what stress is, and you have to experience it more or less regularly.

Here are some smoothies that can combat stress and be beneficial for relaxation.

Recipe 83 – Tomato, Apple & Celery Smoothie

- 3 ripe tomatoes
- 1 apple
- 1 celery

Wash the tomatoes, apple and celery thoroughly. Peel the apple and celery and remove the core from the apple. Blend everything in a blender.

Recipe 84 – Blueberry Apple Smoothie

- 2 apples
- 200 g blueberries

Wash the apples and blueberries thoroughly. Peel the apples and remove the cores.

Blend everything in a blender.

Recipe 85 – Banana, Carrot & Orange Smoothie

- 1 banana
- 1 carrot
- 1 orange

Wash the banana, carrot and orange thoroughly. Peel the banana, carrot and orange and remove the ends of the carrot. Blend everything in a blender.

Recipe 86 – Blueberry, Carrot & Beetroot Smoothie

- 100 g blueberries
- 1 beetroot
- 1 carrot

Wash the beetroot, carrot and blueberries thoroughly. Peel the beetroot and carrot and remove the ends of the carrot. Blend everything in a blender.

Recipe 87 – Apple, Raspberry & Mint Smoothie

- 100 g raspberries
- 2 apples
- A few mint leaves

Wash the raspberries, apples and mint leaves thoroughly. Peel the apples and remove the core.

Blend everything in a blender.

Recipe 88 – Banana, Raspberry & Strawberry Smoothie

- 1 banana
- 7 raspberries
- 7 strawberries

Wash the raspberries, strawberries and banana thoroughly. Peel the banana.

Blend everything in a blender.

Indigestion is the rejection by the digestive system of a recent meal. It is commonly referred to as a "liver attack".

Here are some smoothies that can prevent indigestion and be beneficial for digestion.

Recipe 89 – Tomato, Apple & Celery Smoothie

- 2 ripe tomatoes
- 1 apple
- 1 pear

Wash the tomatoes, apple and pear thoroughly. Peel the apple and pear and remove the cores.

Blend everything in a blender.

Recipe 90 – Pineapple & Beetroot Smoothie

- 1/4 pineapple
- 1 beetroot

Wash the beetroot thoroughly and peel it, as well as the pineapple. Blend everything in a blender. Fresh pineapple absorbs fats and helps to better assimilate meat and fish. Beetroot contains a trace element – rubidium – which is excellent for digestion.

Recipe 91 – Cucumber, Celery & Bell Pepper Smoothie

- 1 cucumber
- 1 celery
- 1 bell pepper

Wash the cucumber, celery and bell pepper thoroughly. Peel the celery and cucumber and remove the core from the pepper.

Blend everything in a blender.

Recipe 92 – Peach, Pitaya & Mango Smoothie

- 1 mango
- 2 peaches
- 1 pitaya

Wash the fruit thoroughly. Peel the mango and pitaya and remove the pits from the peaches and mango.

Blend everything in a blender.

Recipe 93 – Avocado and Cucumber Smoothie

- 1 cucumber
- 1 avocado

Wash the cucumber and avocado thoroughly. Peel them and remove the pit from the avocado.

Blend everything in a blender.

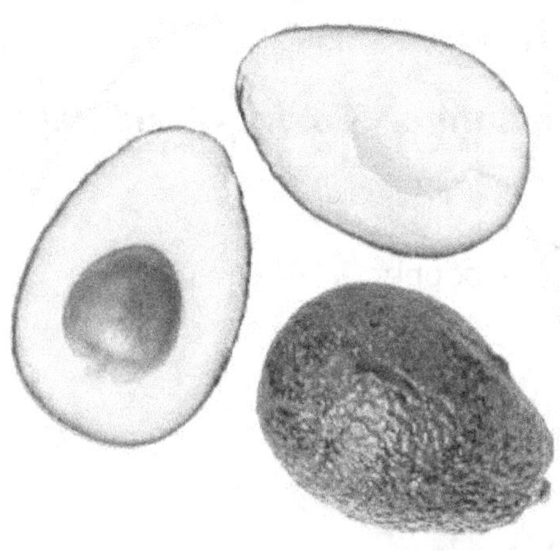

Bowel movements can not only be a cause of stress, but can cause many other problems.

Here are some smoothies that can fight constipation.

Recipe 94 – Orange Pitaya Smoothie

- 1 orange,
- 1 pitaya (dragon fruit)

Wash the fruit thoroughly. Peel them. Watch out for the red-fleshed dragon fruit spot! Blend everything in a blender.

Recipe 95 – Avocado, Orange & Kiwi Smoothie

- 1 avocado,
- 2 kiwis,
- 1 orange

Wash the fruit thoroughly. Peel the kiwis, avocado and orange. Remove the pit from the avocado. Blend everything in a blender.

Recipe 96 – Pear & Apple Smoothie

- 2 apples,
- 2 ripe pears

Wash the apples and pears thoroughly. Peel them and remove the cores. Blend everything in a blender.

Recipe 97 – Melon & Orange Smoothie

- 1 melon
- 1 orange

Wash the melon and orange thoroughly. Peel the melon and orange.

Blend everything in a blender.

Recipe 98 – Mango & Orange Smoothie

- 1 mango
- 1 orange

Wash the mango and orange thoroughly. Peel them and remove the pit from the mango.

Blend everything in a blender.

We have all been victims of diarrhea at one time or another.

Here are some smoothies that can combat it.

Recipe 99 – Banana and Clementine Smoothie

- 1 **unripe** banana
- 3 clementines

Wash the clementines and banana thoroughly. Peel them.

Blend everything in a blender.

Recipe 100 – Melon Pineapple Smoothie

- 1/2 melon
- 1/2 pineapple

Wash the melon thoroughly. Peel the melon and pineapple and cut them into pieces.

Blend everything in a blender.

Recipe 101 – Banana Orange Smoothie

- 1 **unripe banana**
- 1 orange

Wash the fruit thoroughly. Peel them.

Blend everything in a blender.

Credits

- Nutrient icon: Olivier Rebiere, after Magicon
- Close-up photos Smoothies: Freepik.com
- Virtue icon: Olivier Rebiere, after Alexander Skowalsky
- "Ingredients" icon by Becris, Noun Project
- Blender Icon by BomSymbols, Noun Project

Thank you to all the charitable souls who offer free tools and resources on the internet for those who always want to learn and improve!

HOW TO GET THE FREE EBOOK

Did you enjoy this paper book? Would you like to have the electronic version of this guide for free? You can get it on your smartphone or tablet, always at hand and much more eco-friendly!

It's simple: write a review on the platform where you bought your paper book, and send me an email with proof of your review on the website and I'll send you the electronic version right away in your inbox! To do this, just use my email address: cristina.rebiere@gmail.com

I hope to hear from you soon :-)

Cristina

Authors

Cristina and Olivier Rebiere met at the age of seventeen in 1990 in Romania, shortly after the fall of the Berlin Wall and the Romanian Revolution of December 1989.

Since then, these two adventurers of life have had a life full of twists and turns, during which they have developed a taste for travel, entrepreneurship and writing. Their books are useful, practical, and help you get your energy and creativity.

Discover all the books by Cristina & Olivier
https://olivierrebiere.com/e-books-english/